A CONFEDERATE SURGEON'S LETTERS TO HIS WIFE

I0190727

A CONFEDERATE SURGEON'S LETTERS TO HIS WIFE

SPENCER GLASGOW WELCH

*Surgeon, Thirteenth South Carolina Volunteers,
McGowan's Brigade*

WILDSIDE PRESS

Originally published in 1911.
Published by Wildside Press, LLC.
Visit us online at wildsidepress.com.

INTRODUCTION   3

PART I   5

PART II   12

PART III   23

PART IV   34

PART V   43

A CONFEDERATE SURGEON'S LETTERS TO HIS WIFE

INTRODUCTION

Many of the letters written from the battlefield, camp, bivouac or during a halt on the march were lost. It has been necessary to condense those that were received in order to form them into a small volume. This was done by eliminating only the most uninteresting, personal matter that the letters contained and arranging them consecutively. With these exceptions, they are shown here exactly as they were written. This work was done with the greatest care possible by the surgeon's daughter, who is President of the Daughters of the Confederacy for the State of South Carolina and is interested in preserving these letters for their historical value, as they give most vivid pictures of a soldier's life in the Southern army.

PART I

ARRIVAL IN VIRGINIA—BATTLE OF ELLYSON'S MILLS—SEVEN DAYS' FIGHT—WITH STONEWALL JACKSON.

Near Fredericksburg, Va.,
May 16, 1862.

I arrived here this morning about ten o'clock. My trip was all very pleasant, except when I passed through Petersburg and Richmond—both those places are so crowded. The citizens of the latter place are greatly alarmed for fear their city will be captured.

We are close to the enemy now, but there is no certainty of our having a big fight soon. Captain Hunt's men shot at the Yankees this morning while on picket duty. The report about our losing ten men is true. The Yankee cavalry came across the Rappahannock River and captured them.

Our regiment moved after I arrived today and we are now near Summit station in a place where the chinquapin bushes are very thick. The regiments are moved every two or three days to give them practice in moving quickly. All the tents have been taken away from the men, and that, together with the change of climate from the coast of South Carolina to this place, has caused much sickness in our regiment. I will sleep in the medicine tent, a very comfortable place.

It is bedtime now. I will try to write you a longer letter next time. The thought of you and our little George makes me happy, even though I am away off here in Old Virginia.

Hanover County, Va.,
May 27, 1862.

We have just finished a forced march of about forty miles, and have fallen back from near Fredericksburg to within ten miles of Richmond. The Yankees intended to take the Richmond and Potomac Railroad, so we came to reinforce the army already stationed here.

We started last Saturday about dark and continued to travel over the bad, muddy roads all night. We had a very tedious march and did not stop except to get the artillery out of the mire, and at one time to eat and rest a little. Whenever the men would come to mud holes and fords of rivers they would plunge right in without hesitating a moment. This is necessary, because an army must never be allowed to hesitate at anything.

Our brigade consists of the Twelfth, Thirteenth and Fourteenth South Carolina and the Thirty-eighth North Carolina regiments, and is commanded by General Maxey Gregg.

Our division is about fifteen thousand strong and is commanded by General Joseph R. Anderson. It extended several miles, and whenever we would get into a long, straight piece of road where I could look back the sight was most amazing. The compact mass moved four deep, and, with their glittering guns, looked like a river of human beings.

I stood the march finely, and your brother Edwin did not seem to be jaded at all, neither did Billie. Coppock was too sick to move, so we left him behind; but I do not believe he will fall into the hands of the enemy. They are not advancing in that direction. We have been living on crackers and bacon, but I got a fine breakfast this morning on the road. General Gregg and his staff were present and I had the honor of being introduced to them all.

There is little doubt but that we shall get into a fight very soon, possibly before you receive this letter. There must be fighting somewhere on the line now, for I hear the booming of field pieces. We are well prepared for them, and whether we whip them or not they cannot whip us badly.

Take good care of yourself and George.

BATTLE OF ELLYSON'S MILLS

Henrico County, Va.,
June 3, 1862.

Our army whipped the Yankees so badly on Saturday and Sunday (May 28-29) that there was no fighting yesterday. I believe, though, that another fight is going on today, for I hear considerable cannonading, and I saw a balloon up a short while ago.

On Sunday I was sent to Richmond to look after our sick and did not return until late yesterday afternoon. While there I had an opportunity to observe the shocking results of a battle, but, instead of increasing my horror of a battlefield, it made me more anxious than ever to be in a conflict and share its honors. To me every wounded man seemed covered with glory.

Our casualties were certainly very great, for every house which could be had was being filled with the wounded. Even the depots were being filled with them and they came pouring into the hospitals by wagon loads. Nearly all were covered with mud, as they had fought in a swamp most of the time and lay out all night after being wounded. Many of them were but slightly wounded, many others severely, large numbers mortally, and some would die on the road from the battlefield. In every direction the slightly wounded were seen with their arms in slings, their heads tied up, or limping about. One man appeared as if he had been entirely immersed in blood, yet he could walk. Those in the hospitals had received severe flesh wounds or had bones broken, or some vital part penetrated. They did not seem to suffer much and but few ever groaned, but they will suffer when the reaction takes place. I saw one little fellow whose thigh was broken. He was a mere child, but was very cheerful.

Our brigade will move about four miles from here this evening. We occupy the extreme left of Johnson's army and may remain near here for some time, but we cannot tell. Movements of war are very, very uncertain.

Camp near Richmond, Va.,
June 26, 1862.

I returned to camp on Monday because we expected to have a fight. Our brigade was ordered away last night with two days' rations, but I am left behind with the sick. There are a great many sick men in the hospitals and they are dying by the thousands. Our regiment has lost about one hundred men since we came to Virginia.

The enemy threw shells all about our camp yesterday and killed two horses, but only one man. It was a great day between our batteries and those of the enemy. They fired all day long, but as it was all at long taw little damage was done. I went out this morning to view the enemy, and could see them and their breast-works very distinctly.

Since I began writing this letter I hear a terrific cannonading on the left wing of our army, and I believe the battle has opened. I am informed that General Jackson is about there and that a fight will certainly take place this week.

You must be cheerful and take things easy, because I believe the war will soon be ended.

SEVEN DAYS' FIGHT AROUND RICHMOND.

Camp near Richmond, Va.,
June 29, 1862.

I was correct in my last letter to you when I predicted that the great battle had commenced (Chickahominy or Gaines Mills). The conflict raged with great fury after I finished writing, and it lasted from three o'clock until ten that night. The cannonading was so continuous at one time that I could scarcely hear the musketry at all. There was one incessant boom and roar for three hours without any cessation. Next morning (28th) the battle began anew, but there was not nearly so much cannonading, because our men rushed upon the Yankees and took their cannon. The musketry, though, was terrific. It reminded me of myriads of hail-stones falling upon a house top. I could see the smoke and the bombs burst in the air, and could hear the shouts of our men as they would capture the Yankee batteries.

Our brigade took the advance in the morning when the battle commenced, and after we routed them we did not get a chance to fight them again until we had driven them about eight or ten miles from where we started them. They rallied there and made a stand, but our troops rushed at them again and drove them to—God only knows where! A Yankee officer (a prisoner) told me they had no idea General Jackson was anywhere about here, and he acknowledged that General McClellan was completely outwitted. I tell you the Yankee "Napoleon" has been badly defeated.

Our colonel surprised his men by his bravery. My brother Billie is greatly mortified because he was too sick to be in the fight. He is still hardly able to walk. Our regiment had eight killed and forty wounded. Orr's Regiment and the First South Carolina were badly cut up in an attempt to capture a battery. (The former had 81 killed and 234 wounded, and the latter 20 killed and 125 wounded).

I was on the ground yesterday (Saturday) where some of the hardest fighting took place. The dead were lying everywhere and were very thick in some places. One of our regiments had camped in some woods there and the men were lying among the dead Yankees and seemed unconcerned.

The most saddening sight was the wounded at the hospitals, which were in various places on the battlefield. Not only are the houses full, but even the yards are covered with them. There are so many that most of them are much neglected. The people of Richmond are hauling them away as fast as possible. At one place I saw the Yankee wounded and their own surgeon attending to them. There are no crops or fences anywhere, and I saw nothing which had escaped the Yankees except one little Guinea fowl. I thought our army was bad enough, but the country over which the Yankees have been looks like some barren waste. On my way to the battlefield I met a negro who recognized me and told me that your brother Edwin was wounded in the breast and had gone to Richmond. I fear there is some truth in it.

WITH STONEWALL JACKSON

Near Orange Court House, Va.,
August 12, 1862.

While we are resting a little I will endeavor to write you a few lines. We have been moving about continuously since I wrote to you on the 8th inst., and have had some hard times, I assure you. Most of our hard marching has been during the night, but much of it has been in the heat of the day. We have had nothing to eat but crackers and bacon, and not nearly enough of that.

We first (on the 9th inst.) marched up into Culpeper County, and were within two miles of the battlefield (of Cedar Mountain). It was a brilliant victory for us, as two of their dead to one of ours were left on the field. On the way we met a great many prisoners, who were lively and jocose and seemed glad they were taken.

The weather has been fine, although very hot. We had one hard shower of rain, and everybody stood and took it, as there was nothing else we could do. Tell your brother he should be glad he was wounded, for it has saved him many great hardships. I never murmur at these trials, though, as long as I can have good health.

Last night we began falling back. I suppose it was some strategic move and that we will continue these active operations until a decisive fight takes place. General Jackson will not be outgeneraled, and I believe he is sure to defeat Pope. I saw him (Jackson) this morning. He is a very ordinary look-ing man.

I would like to write you a longer letter, but have not the time. We are now drawing rations, and as soon as we get our meat boiled will start again. I must close, as preparations are being made to leave, so good-bye for this time.

Orange County, Va.,
August 18, 1862.

On leaving our last camp we first went back five miles in a northerly di-rection to Orange Court House, and we thought Jackson intended to take us over the same road we had fallen back on a few days before; but from there we took the road to Fredericksburg. Then everyone said we were going to Fredericksburg. That was a mistake also, for after going about ten miles we turned to the left and went three miles toward the Rapidan River, and have stopped at this place. It is believed that Jackson intended to cross the river and flank Pope, and that the Yankees got wind of it. They were on a mountain and may have seen our large force moving. Jackson is a general who is full of resources, and if he fails in one plan he will try another.

The men stood the march better than at any previous time. The health of the brigade has improved since we are where we can breathe the pure mountain air. This beautiful country, with its mountains and rolling hills, is enough to make any sick man feel better. We all sleep out in the open air— officers as well as privates—although the weather is becoming quite cool and signs of autumn begin to appear. The crops of corn are magnificent and are almost matured, but wherever our army goes, roasting ears and green apples suffer. I have often read of how armies are disposed to pillage and plunder, but could never conceive of it before. Whenever we stop for twenty-four hours every corn field and orchard within two or three miles is completely stripped. The troops not only rob the fields, but they go to the houses and insist on being fed, until they eat up everything about a man's premises which can be eaten. Most of them pay for what they get at the houses, and are charged exorbitant prices, but a hungry soldier will give all he has for something to eat, and will then steal when hunger again harasses him. When in health and tormented by hunger he thinks of little else besides home and something to eat. He does not seem to dread the fatiguing marches and arduous duties.

A wounded soldier who has been in Jackson's army for a long time told me his men had but one suit of clothes each, and whenever a suit became very dirty the man would pull it off and wash it and then wait until it dried. I believe this to be a fact, because when I see Jackson's old troop on the march none have any load to carry except a blanket, and many do not even have a blanket; but they always appear to be in fine spirits and as healthy and clean as any of our men. The force we have here now is a mammoth one. I am told that Lee and Johnson are both here, and I am anxious for our army to engage Pope. Whenever we start on a march I am impatient to go on and fight it out, for we are confident we can whip the enemy.

We are now cooking up two days' rations and are ordered to have them in our haversacks and be ready to move at sundown, but we may not go at that time, because we sometimes receive such orders and then do not leave for a day or two. I will write again whenever I have a chance.

Culpeper County, Va.,
August 24, 1862.

Our army pursued Pope's to this place last week. We are now on the west side of North Fork of the Rappahannock River, while Pope is on the other side. Each army is trying to get the advantage of the other, and it is difficult for either to cross the river while the other opposes it. It is evident that we shall have a tremendous fight in a few days. General Lee is here with us, for I saw him pass by. We have just cooked up two days' rations and are expecting every minute to leave here.

I saw a pretty little fight a few days ago when I was far in the rear with the ambulance train, and it was by the merest chance that the train was not cut off from the main force and captured. General Hood with his staff was reconnoitering, and was fired upon by the Yankees, who were under the cover of some woods a little distance from the road. A Texas brigade happened to be passing and was sent against them, and whipped them badly.

There has been quite an amount of rain recently, but we have no tents, nor even anything in the shape of tents.

I have a chance to send this to Gordonsville, and as the bearer is about to leave I must close. I could write you a long letter if I had time, so good-bye for now.

PART II

MANASSAS AND SHARPSBURG (ANTIETAM)—BATTLE OF FREDERICKSBURG—IN CAMP NEAR FREDERICKSBURG.

Ox Hill, Va.,
September 3, 1862.

I was in the battle at Manassas and made several very narrow escapes. I had to go on the field there, although it was Dr. Kilgore's place to go, and not mine, but he was afraid to go. On Monday (September 1) at this place I came very near being killed; for a bombshell barely did miss me and burst right at me. I stood the late terrible march surprisingly well, but I have learned what hunger and hardships are. I would often lie down at night on the bare ground without a blanket or anything else to cover with and would wonder what my dear wife would think if she could see me lying there. We have had some dreadful sufferings, especially on these forced marches. The fatigue and the pangs of hunger were fearful.

We marched fast all day Monday and all day Tuesday (August 25 and 26) and until late Tuesday night, when we bivouacked in a field of tall grass near Bristow Station. Bob Land spread his wet horse blanket on a bare spot, and we lay on it and covered with his blanket and went to sleep without supper. The country was a waste, and I heard no sound of a chicken, cow or dog during the night.

The next morning (Wednesday) we got up before day and marched fast to Manassas Junction, and almost kept up with the cavalry. We found sutlers' stores and trainloads of flour and meat, and we captured a few prisoners. I went into a sutler's tent and got three days' rations of ham, crackers and salt. Before noon we started towards Washington, and after marching three or four miles we marched back to Manassas Junction again late that afternoon and found many prisoners and negroes there, who were all sent away towards Groveton. We staid there that night, and all the cars and everything were set on fire about the same time. We were very tired, and all day lay down on the ground, but I remained awake for some time watching the fire, which burned fiercely. Thursday morning (28th) we marched nearly to Centreville, and from there towards Groveton, and Ewell's command got into a fight late that afternoon on our right. We remained there and bivouacked in the oak forest where our brigade fought next day.

Next morning (Friday) we had breakfast, and I ate with Adjutant Goggans. Our command then took position in the woods near the cut of an unfinished railroad and sent out skirmishers, who soon retreated and fell back on the main line. The Yankee line came up quite near and fired into us from our right, and Goggans was shot through the body. I remained some distance in rear of our line and saw Mike Bowers, Dave Suber and two other men bringing someone back on a litter, and I said: "Mike, who is that?" and he said: "Goggans," just as they tumbled him down. I looked at him as he was gasping his last, and he died at once. Then the wounded who could walk began to come back, and those who could not were brought to me on litters. I did all I could for them until the ambulances could carry them to the field infirmary, and this continued until late in the afternoon.

I saw an Irishman from South Carolina bringing a wounded Irishman from Pennsylvania back and at the same time scolding him for fighting us. Colonel McGowan came limping back, shot through the thigh, but he refused to ride, and said: "Take men who are worse hurt than I am." Colonel Marshall and Lieutenant-Colonel Leadbetter were brought back mortally wounded.

Shells came over to us occasionally as if thrown at our reserves, and would burst among the men and overhead, but they paid no attention to them and kept very quiet. I did not hear anyone say one word. An occasional spent ball fell near by and one knocked up the dust close to me, but the trees were thick and stopped most of the bullets short of us. The Yankees charged us seven times during the day and were driven back every time. Their lines were always preceded by skirmishers. One ran into the railroad cut and sat down, and Jim Wood shot him dead.

Our brigade was not relieved until about four o'clock. They had been fighting all day and their losses were very heavy. I saw General Fields, commanding a Virginia brigade, ride in on our left to relieve us, and I then went back to the field infirmary, where I saw large numbers of wounded lying on the ground as thick as a drove of hogs in a lot. They were groaning and crying out with pain, and those shot in the bowels were crying for water. Jake Fellers had his arm amputated without chloroform. I held the artery and Dr. Huot cut it off by candle light. We continued to operate until late at night and attended to all our wounded. I was very tired and slept on the ground.

We did nothing Saturday morning (30th). There were several thousand prisoners near by, and I went where they were and talked with some of them. Dr. Evans, the brigade surgeon, went to see General Lee, and General Lee told him the battle would begin that morning at about ten o'clock and would cease in about two hours, which occurred exactly as he said. Our brigade was not engaged, and we spent the day sending the wounded to Richmond.

Early Sunday morning (31st) we started away, and I passed by where Goggans' body lay. Near him lay the body of Captain Smith of Spartanburg. Both were greatly swollen and had been robbed of their trousers and shoes by our own soldiers, who were ragged and bare-footed, and did it from necessity. We passed on over the battlefield where the dead and wounded Yankees lay. They had fallen between the lines and had remained there without attention since Friday. We marched all day on the road northward and traveled about twelve miles.

The next morning (September 1) we continued our march towards Fairfax Court House, and had a battle late that afternoon at Ox Hill during a violent thunderstorm. Shell were thrown at us and one struck in the road and burst within three or four feet of me. Several burst near Colonel Edwards as he rode along, but he did not pay the slightest attention to them. There were flashes and keen cracks of lightning near by and hard showers of rain fell. The Yankees had a strong position on a hill on the right side of the road, but our men left the road and I could see them hurrying up the hill with skirmishers in advance of the line.

I went into a horse lot and established a field infirmary, and saw an old lady and her daughter fleeing from a cottage and crossing the lot in the rain. The old lady could not keep up and the daughter kept stopping and urging her mother to hurry. The bullets were striking all about the yard of their house.

Lieutenant Leopard from Lexington was brought back to me with both his legs torn off below the knees by a shell, and another man with part of his arm torn off, but neither Dr. Kenedy, Dr. Kilgore nor our medical wagon was with us, and I had nothing with me to give them but morphine. They both died during night. The battle continued till night came on and stopped it. We filled the carriage house, barn and stable with our wounded, but I could do but little for them. Colonel Edwards was furious, and told me to tell the other doctors "for God's sake to keep with their command."

After doing all I could for the wounded, my brother, my servant Wilson, and myself went into the orchard and took pine poles from a fence and spread them on the wet ground to sleep on. I discovered a small chicken roosting in a peach tree and caught it, and Wilson skinned it and broiled it, and it was all we three had to eat that day. Wilson got two good blankets off the battlefield with "U. S." on them, and we spread one on the poles and covered with the other.

The next morning the Yankees were gone. Their General, Kearney, was killed and some of their wounded fell into our hands. The two other doctors with our medical supplies did not get there until morning, and many of our wounded died during the night. I found one helpless man lying under a blanket between two men who were dead.

We drew two days' rations of crackers and bacon about ten o'clock, and I ate them all and was still very hungry. I walked over on the hill and saw a few dead Yankees. They had become stiff, and one was lying on his back with an arm held up. I picked up a good musket and carried it back with me to the house and gave it to the young lady I saw running away the day before. She thanked me for it, and seemed very much pleased to have it as a memento of the battle.

Late that afternoon we drew rations again, and I ate everything without satisfying my hunger. A soldier came from another command and said he heard I had some salt, and he offered me a shoulder of fresh pork for some. Wilson cooked it and I ate it without crackers, but was still hungry. During the night I became very sick from overeating, and next morning when the regiment left I was too sick to march. Billie, Mose Cappock, Billy Caldwell and myself all got sick from the same cause. We are all sleeping in the carriage house, and I have sent Wilson out into the country to get something for us to eat.

We hope to be able to go on and catch up with the regiment in a day or two. It has gone in the direction of Harper's Ferry.

Charlestown, Jefferson County, W. Va.,
September 24, 1862.

I have not written to you in three or four weeks, because there has been no mail between us and Richmond. I have seen sights since then, I assure you. If I should tell you what our army has endured recently you could hardly believe it. Thousands of the men now have almost no clothes and no sign of a blanket nor any prospect of getting one, either. Thousands have had no shoes at all, and their feet are now entirely bare. Most of our marches were on graveled turnpike roads, which were very severe on the barefooted men and cut up their feet horribly. When the poor fellows could get rags they would tie them around their feet for protection. I have seen the men rob the dead of their shoes and clothing, but I cannot blame a man for doing a thing which is almost necessary in order to preserve his own life. I passed Goggans' body two days after he was killed at Manassas, and there the poor fellow lay, robbed like all the others. (Do not say anything about this, for his family might hear of it.)

I was sick for one week at a private house, and did not catch up with our regiment until the day after the battle at Sharpsburg, Maryland. Doubtless you have learned how our regiment suffered in the battle, and it is useless for me to tell you of the shocking scenes I have witnessed. Billie was in the battle at Shepherds-town. Our men put it right into the Yankees there when they had them in the river.

I do not know where our regiment is at present, but have heard that it is near Martinsburg. My brother was well when I last saw him. He and I have three flannel shirts between us, and I have some other very good clothes. I have but one pair of socks, and they are nearly worn out. I had a good pair, but some one stole them.

I am now here at a hospital with our wounded, and will remain until they are well enough to be moved away. The Yankees came near enough the other day to throw several shells into the town, but they did no harm except to wound a little boy. They are certainly fanatical. As much as we whip them, they are not disposed to give up. The people here—especially the women—hate them bitterly.

I am boarding with the widow of the late Judge Douglass of Virginia, and as I have plenty of everything which is good to eat I am beginning to fatten, but will soon lose it when I start on the march again. The people are overwhelming in their kindness to our wounded, and bring them every dainty.

I could write you some interesting letters now, but I have very little hope of this one getting through to you. I do wish so much I could hear from you and George; that worries me more than everything else put together, although I have seen so much recently which was shocking and horrible that I am hard to worry about anything. If I am spared to get home I shall be a wiser, if not a better, man. So good-bye for the present, my dear wife.

Berkeley County, Va.,
October 8, 1862.

When I left Charlestown yesterday morning the weather was delightful and I felt so buoyant and fresh that it caused me to walk too fast, and today I am very sore and stiff. I found four letters from you, and they were a treat, for I had had no intelligence from you since July. I never get homesick in camp when I hear that you and George are well.

Our army has been here for three weeks. We are fourteen miles from Charlestown and ten miles northeast of Winchester. There is smallpox in Winchester, and General Lee has ordered the entire army vaccinated.

The weather is dry and pleasant and the men are in better health than I have ever seen them. This rich valley is full of provisions and the army is well fed. It is said that vast quantities of provisions of every kind are being sent from this valley into the interior to prevent the Yankees from getting them, and that when we have eaten out everything in this region we shall retire toward the interior. We have at present no prospect whatever of a fight. If our victory at Sharpsburg had been complete, doubtless we should now be in Pennsylvania.

Dr. Chapman got sick at Richmond, and we have heard nothing from him since. He had become so disagreeable that we had enough of him.

I have tried to be very faithful to my duty since I have been in the army, and I get along finely with the other doctors.

I will close this letter, so good-bye, my dear wife and little boy.

Berryville, Clark County, Va.,
November 13, 1862.

Our brigade is now camped in the suburbs of Berryville and is doing picket duty; however, in three days more another brigade will relieve us. The rest of the division is within five miles of Winchester. There seems to be no prospect of a fight at this time, although our men continue to take prisoners occasionally. The largest number brought in at one time was 104.

The weather is still quite cold, but the health of the brigade remains good. But few men reported sick this morning. We still hear of a case of smallpox occasionally, but the army is well vaccinated and I am satisfied that we are all immune. We have plenty to eat. For breakfast this morning we had biscuit (and they were shortened too), fried bacon and fried cabbage. For dinner we had boiled beef and dumplings, with biscuit and boiled eggs. Dr. Kilgore and I dined in Berryville yesterday with a Dr. Counsellor. The dinner was fine and the table was graced by his charming wife.

I still have about thirty dollars, but our quartermaster has gone to Richmond to get several months' pay for us. Please send my suit to me, for I wish to give the one I am now wearing to my servant, Wilson. He also needs a pair of shoes. In your last letter you ask if I have the night-cap which your aunt made for me. I lost it one morning before day, when preparing for battle. Take good care of George.

THE RETURN TO FREDERICKSBURG

Camp near Fredericksburg, Va.,
December 4, 1862.

We traveled 175 miles from the Valley to this place in twelve days, and are now encamped upon precisely the same spot we were occupying when we left this region last spring. Our march was the least disagreeable of any I have experienced, because the weather was very cold and we traveled during the day only. We were well fed also, compared with our other marches. We had rain but once and snow twice. Many of the men were barefooted and the march was terrible for them. Billie, Ed and I stood it first-rate and none of us lagged behind once. By a mere chance we got our clothing at Orange Court House. We feel very grateful to you and the others for your trouble and expense for us. My suit fits as well as I could wish, and everyone admires it. Wilson had his knapsack stolen the first night after we got the clothes. He is very careless, and so is Billie. Unless one is extremely careful everything he has will be stolen from him in camp. Half of the men in the army seem to have become thieves.

We have an enormous force concentrated here now. Nearly all the men are well clothed, but some few are not. We still have a few barefooted men because their feet are too large for the Government shoes. The health of the troops continues fine. Last summer never less than two hundred men reported sick every morning in our regiment, and now there are never more than twelve or fifteen cases.

I doubt our having any more fighting this winter, as such weather as this puts a stop to all military operations. The enemy cannot advance on us nor can we advance on them. I think we surely will go into winter quarters soon, for it is folly for us to be lying out as we are. We have good health, it is true, but it is extremely unpleasant.

I may have an opportunity to send you some more money soon, and you may spend it if you wish, for it may be worthless when the war is over.

George will be one year old on the seventh.

BATTLE OF FREDERICKSBURG

Camp near Fredericksburg, Va.,
December 24, 1862.

The Yankees seem loath to make another advance since the good whipping we gave them here on the thirteenth in the battle of Fredericksburg. Milton Bossardt's company went into the fight with forty men, and thirty of them were killed or wounded. He escaped very narrowly. A hole was shot through his hat and one of his shoe heels was shot off. Pick Stevens never shuns a fight. He goes boldly into them all.

I will not write you about the battle, for you must have seen enough in the newspapers concerning it. According to their own newspaper accounts, the Yankees were defeated much worse than we at first thought they were.

Some of us sent out today and got some eggs, and are going to have an egg-nog tonight, so you see we are trying to have some enjoyment for Christmas if we are out here in the woods. The Government is trying to help us, for we drew several extra good things today.

You must keep in good spirits. I will get home some of these days yet. I may surprise you.

IN CAMP NEAR FREDERICKSBURG

Camp on Rappahannock River,
Spottsylvania County, Va.,
December 28, 1862.

The weather during Christmas has been as warm and pleasant as I ever saw it at the same season in South Carolina, but this morning it was quite clear and cold. I like the cold weather here, for we have such fine health. It is seldom that we have a man to die now. Our army was in better fighting trim at the battle of Fredericksburg than at any time since the war began, and it is still in the same condition. It does not seem possible to defeat this army now with General Lee at its head.

The Yankees are certainly very tired of this war. All the prisoners I have talked with express themselves as completely worn out and disgusted with it. Our regiment was on picket at the river a few days ago and the Yankee pickets were on the opposite bank. There is no firing between pickets now. It is forbidden in both armies. The men do not even have their guns loaded. The two sides talk familiarly with each other, and the Yankees say they are very anxious to have peace and get home.

Edwin and James Allen dined with me yesterday and said it was the best meal they had partaken of since they left home. We had fried tripe, chicken and dumplings, shortened biscuits, tea which was sweetened, and peach pie. Ed slept with me and took breakfast with me this morning. He thought my quarters very good for camp.

I have a pocketful of money now, and while there is a dollar of it left you can have all you wish. I would certainly like so very much to be with you, but it will never do for our country to be sacrificed in order that our selfish desires for comfort and ease may be gratified. It is everyone's duty to lend a helping hand to his country and never abandon his post of duty because a few who have no patriotism do so.

While I write I hear Chaplain Beauschelle preaching at a tremendous rate. He seems to think everyone is very deaf. I should prefer to hear some ludicrous old negro preacher, for that would afford me some amusement. To save my life I cannot think of anything more to write, so good-bye, my dear wife. Take good care of George.

Yesterday was a very wet day, but we can keep fairly comfortable with the little Yankee tents we have captured during the summer campaign and with those which have been issued to us. Wood is very plentiful where we are now encamped and we have rousing fires. We have been blessed so far this winter in regard to weather. We have become so accustomed to the cold that we do not mind it, and you will be surprised when I tell you that for the last two nights I have slept part of the time without any cover at all. When I was at home I would have a fresh cold every two or three weeks during the winter, but now, with all our exposure, I never have a cold, and I believe it is because I am in the same temperature all the time.

Everything is very quiet here, and we have no prospect at all of a fight. The Yankee forces are so large that we cannot expect to gain more decided victories over them. All we can do is to hold them in check until they are discouraged and worn out.

General Lee grants furloughs now to two at a time from each company, and I may soon have a chance to get home. I am very anxious to see George. He must be very attractive, but we must not dote on him or anything else which is earthly. When you write tell me all about some of his little capers.

February 15, 1863.
(Sunday.)

This is a very unpleasant day, but I am comfortable in my tent by the fire. The snow and cold do not make it as disagreeable for us as one would naturally suppose, because we have become accustomed to it. The men seem to enjoy the snow very much. About two weeks ago it was more than one foot deep, and some of the regiments met in regular battle order and had snow fights with each other, and they would yell at a great rate. The bitter cold of winter does not compare in severity with the hard marching of a summer campaign, and I should prefer six winters in camp to one summer on the march.

I saw the Medical Director yesterday at Hamilton's Crossing. He was very pleasant, and assigned me to the Thirteenth South Carolina Regiment without any hesitation. In going to General Lee's headquarters I could see the Yankee camps distinctly, on the other side of the river. I could even see their forces drilling. Their camps are very extensive indeed, and the vast numbers of white tents which stretch across the plains give it the appearance of a great city. This weather puts a stop to Burnside's advance, but I have no fear of defeat when he does advance.

I went to the depot at Guinea's Station and got the box from home. I found it filled with everything which is good to eat, and I would not care to fare any better than at present. I had Edwin, Jim Allen and Ben Strother to take dinner with me the next day. They praised the dinner very much and ate only as soldiers can. I must have all three of them to come again in a day or two.

Two years ago from last Friday you and I were married, and how changed is the scene since then! Little did we think that devastation and distress would so soon spread over the entire land. War seems to be a natural occurrence. It has been our misfortune to experience it, and there is nothing we can do but endure it philosophically and try to become resigned to it.

When you write tell me all the little particulars about George. I dreamed last night of being at home, but thought he would have nothing to do with me and treated me like an entire stranger.

Camp near Rappahannock River, Va.,
March 5, 1863.

Edwin, Jim Allen and Ben Strother took dinner with me yesterday, and I think I gave them a pretty good dinner for camp. We had biscuit, excellent ham, fried potatoes, rice, light bread, butter, stewed fruit and sugar. They ate heartily, as soldiers always do. Edwin is not suffering from his wound, but on account of it he is privileged to have his baggage hauled.

A man was shot near our regiment last Sunday for desertion. It was a very solemn scene. The condemned man was seated on his coffin with his hands tied across his breast. A file of twelve soldiers was brought up to within six feet of him, and at the command a volley was fired right into his breast. He was hit by but one ball, because eleven of the guns were loaded with powder only. This was done so that no man can be certain that he killed him. If he was, the thought of it might always be painful to him. I have seen men marched through the camps under guard with boards on their backs which were labeled, "I am a coward," or "I am a thief," or "I am a shirker from battle," and I saw one man tied hand and foot astride the neck of a cannon and exposed to view for sixteen hours. These severe punishments seem necessary to preserve discipline.

We have no prospect of a fight now whatever, but if the weather continues dry and pleasant it may come soon. We are too well entrenched for them to attack us here, but it is hard to tell what these crazy, fanatical Yankees intend to do.

Our troops are all in fine health. We seldom send a man to the hospital now, but when we were on the Chickahominy River near Richmond we sent from five to twelve each day. I trust we will be exposed to no greater danger in the future than the bullets, for they do not compare in destructiveness with disease. Captain Hunt's company has lost seven men from bullets and twenty-five from disease, and in most of the companies the difference is greater than this.

The weather for the last three or four days has been very windy and blustering and characteristic of March. It was intensely cold last night, but today the sun broke out and it is pleasant.

I am anxious to see George. I know he is a charming little fellow.

Camp near Rappahannock River, Va.,
April 5, 1863.

The weather has been more disagreeable since the beginning of April than at any previous time this winter. The wind has blown almost incessantly and furiously at times. Today is one of the windiest and most disagreeable that I ever saw. It is awful. I hope the wind will subside by night, or I am afraid it will blow my tent down. Yesterday when it was nearly night snow began falling, and with it there was a hurricane of wind, which continued through the night, and was terrific at times. I expected the tent to come down on Billie and me every moment, but it stood the gale finely, although it kept up a horrible flapping all night. The wind is still blowing today and the snow is several inches deep. Such weather as this will delay "Fighting Joe" Hooker's movements for some time, and it is so much the better for us.

There is now some scurvy in the army, which is caused by a lack of a vegetable diet. It is not serious yet and is easily cured if the men can get vegetables to eat.

We received orders from General Lee to be ready for an active campaign on the first of the month, by getting rid of all our surplus baggage. About one week ago I saw a Yankee balloon up on the other side of the river, and was told that General Lee had one up at the same time, but I did not see it. I do not believe we shall have so severe a campaign this spring and summer as we had last year, but I am more than willing to endure all the hardships again to be as victorious as we were then. You need have no apprehension that this army will ever meet with defeat while commanded by General Lee. General Jackson is a strict Presbyterian, but he is rather too much of a Napoleon Bonaparte in my estimation. Lee is the man, I assure you.

Dr. Kilgore and a great many others are extremely tired of this war, and he has succeeded in getting transferred to Macon, Ga. The surgeon who has taken his place is Dr. Tyler, a son of the former President of the United States. When the Thirteenth Regiment was formed there were six doctors and two bookkeepers in the medical department, and now every one of them has gone but myself.

I am glad that George is so bright and intelligent.

PART III

BATTLE OF CHANCELLORSVILLE—MARCH TO PENNSYLVANIA—INVASION OF PENNSYLVANIA —RETREAT FROM GETTYSBURG—BATTLE OF GETTYSBURG.

BATTLE OF CHANCELLORSVILLE

Camp Gregg, Va.,
May 7, 1863.

We have just returned from the field of the great battle. It was a complete victory for us. It was a terrible fight. Our brigade charged on their breastworks and took them. Edwin and Billie were both in it. Edwin was not touched, but Billie had two bullet holes through his clothes. He was not hurt, though. We have had a very hard time of it for seven or eight days. My mind and body are so worn out that I will not write any more, but will tomorrow or next day. When I write again I will write the particulars. Edwin, Billie and I are in good health.

good-bye for the present.

23

On Saturday morning (the 2d inst.) I received an order to ship the wounded to Richmond, store our medical supplies and follow the wagon train to Chancellorsville. I carried the chest of supplies to a large house, which Stonewall Jackson had for his headquarters, and was met at the door by a young lady who was whistling. She appeared to be quite aristocratic and was very courteous to us.

We started late in the afternoon, and I marched with the wagon train all night. It was carrying rations and did not stop once. Most of the road was through woods, but we could see well enough to march all night, and in some places there was mud, but no wagon stalled.

Just before daylight I saw a dead Yankee lying close to the right of the road. I did not know until then that there had been any fighting. I knew our command left that morning, but had heard no firing and knew nothing of what had taken place. Just as it was getting light the Yankees threw shells, which burst about the wagons, and the teamsters became excited and began whipping their horses and hurrying to get away; but a quartermaster at once commanded them to keep quiet and get away in good order, and the excitement ceased. The fighting then began just as soon as they could see.

I went on hunting for the field infirmary, and when I found it our wounded were coming back and a few had been brought back before I got there, and I at once went to work assisting in amputations, and continued at it all day and until late at night.

Jackson's men came in from the rear on Saturday night and drove the Yankees from their breastworks and occupied them that morning (Sunday, May 3). The Yankees came back early and tried to retake them, and I could hear them fighting furiously for several hours. We knew nothing of Stonewall Jackson's being shot the night before.

During the assault Colonel Edwards walked along on top of the works waving his sword to encourage his men, and was shot through the shoulder. When he was brought back I helped him out of the ambulance and expressed sympathy for him, which caused him to shed tears, but he said nothing. Colonel James Perrin was brought back shot through the body and in great agony, and General McGowan was struck below the knee while standing upon the works. I saw my brother once during the day bringing a wounded man back.

Captain McFall and Lieutenant Mike Bowers came back looking for stragglers, and found four young men who were known to be cowards, but who were always great braggarts after a battle was over. They all pretended to be sick, but I could see no indications of it, and they were marched off, but, before reaching the works, one of them slipped away, although the fighting had ended.

After all the wounded were attended to I was very tired and went to sleep late that night in a tent. I would wake up cold during the night and reach out for a jug of whiskey and take a swallow and go back to sleep again.

The next morning (Monday the 4th) we did nothing. Several handsome young Yankee surgeons in fine uniforms came over with a white flag, and I went to where they were attending to their wounded. While there I talked with a wounded man from Ohio, and saw one of our soldiers cut a forked limb from a tree and make a crutch for a Yankee who was wounded in the foot. The unfed horses of a Yankee cavalry regiment had been hitched to the trees near by and had gnawed off all the bark within their reach.

We stayed there for three days until the Yankees crossed back over the Rappahannock River, and then we marched back to Moss Neck in the daytime in peace and found our tents standing where we left them.

Hospital near Hamilton's Crossing, Va.,
June 12, 1863.

Our corps is lying in line of battle in the trenches, and has been for six days. The Yankees are still on this side of the river. The picket lines are within speaking distance of each other and we exchange newspapers with them every day. I went there this morning and was never before so close to the enemy when in a hostile attitude. I saw the New York Illustrated News , and will try to get a copy to send to you. I stay out on the field with the troops during the day, but come back to the hospital at night.

Chaplain Beauchelle messes with Dr. Tyler and me while his messmates are out in the line. He and Tyler sleep together. Tyler is one of the most wicked and profane men I ever knew, but he is a very intelligent man and is generous and high-minded. His father educated him for the ministry, and he and the chaplain argue on Scripture at night. It is highly amusing, for he is hard to handle in an argument on Scripture.

I am told that all of our army has gone in the direction of Manassas except our corps (A. P. Hill's), which was formerly Stonewall Jackson's. It consists of Pender's, Heath's and Anderson's divisions, and is about twenty-five or thirty thousand strong. We can take care of any Yankee force which may come at us in our present position. I have not seen Edwin in two days, and suppose he is strengthening the entrenchments here and there where they may chance to be defective.

My father wrote me that George was the liveliest child he ever saw, and that it was a matter of rejoicing when you and George were seen coming.

The Yankees have all gone back on the other side of the river, and we have left our entrenchments and taken up camp in the rear. I think we shall not remain here long, but I do not know what we shall do next. The enemy seem to have left Fredericksburg. If we do not move tomorrow I may write again.

I am getting very anxious to hear from you and George.

Between Front Royal and Winchester, Va.,
June 21, 1863.

We are in the Valley of Virginia again and are now within ten miles of Winchester. You cannot imagine how delighted the Valley people are at our appearance. The ladies wave their handkerchiefs from every little farm-house we pass and cheer us onward. Such sights are enough to make any-one feel enthusiastic. As we marched through Front Royal this morning the people were in ecstasies and our bands played lively airs for them, although it is Sunday.

In coming from Fredericksburg here we have taken a much shorter route than the one we took in going from here to that place last fall. Since we left Fredericksburg last week we have not traveled more than one hundred miles, but we traveled 175 miles by the other route. We camped on the top of the mountains last night. The night before we did not go into camp until about ten o'clock, and then it began to rain furiously. We were in an open grass field and so we had to stand up and take it. It was a very heavy rain and the night was the worst I ever experienced. I sat up the entire night on a rock and kept dry with an oilcloth. Few men were so fortunate as to have so good a place to sit on as a rock. I am willing to endure almost anything, or to be deprived of almost everything, if we can have the pleasure of getting into Pennsylvania and letting the Yankees feel what it is to be invaded.

Our army is very large now, and if we get into Maryland or Pennsylvania and Hooker engages us you may be certain that he will be severely whipped. General Lee and his army are bent on it. Our troops are in fine health and I have never before seen them get along half so well on a march. Not a man has given out since the rain. I believe they will fight better than they have ever done, if such a thing could be possible. I feel fine and have stood the march admirably. We have had plenty of meat and bread to eat since we started, and I got some good rich milk this morning at Front Royal.

From where I am writing this letter I can look around me and see one of the most beautiful and fertile countries. I do wish you could see it. My ser-vant has gone to a farmhouse, and he stays so long that I believe he is hav-ing something cooked.

I shall write to you as often as I can; so good-bye to you and George.

Franklin County, Pa.,
June 28, 1863.

We are in Yankeedom this time, for certain, and a beautiful and magnificent country it is too. Since we started we have traveled about fifteen miles a day, resting at night and drawing rations plentifully and regularly. We are about fifteen miles over the Pennsylvania and Maryland line and within seven miles of Chambersburg. We are resting today (Sunday) and will get to Harrisburg in three more days if we go there.

We hear nothing of Hooker's army at all, but General Lee knows what he is about. This is certainly a grand move of his, and if any man can carry it out successfully he can, for he is cautious as well as bold.

We are taking everything we need—horses, cattle, sheep, flour, groceries and goods of all kinds, and making as clean a sweep as possible. The people seem frightened almost out of their senses. They are nearly all agricultural people and have everything in abundance that administers to comfort. I have never yet seen any country in such a high state of cultivation. Such wheat I never dreamed of, and so much of it! I noticed yesterday that scarcely a horse or cow was to be seen. The free negroes are all gone, as well as thousands of the white people. My servant, Wilson, says he "don't like Pennsylvania at all," because he "sees no black folks."

I have never seen our army so healthy and in such gay spirits. How can they be whipped? Troops have so much better health when on the march. I must say that I have enjoyed this tramp. The idea of invading the Yankees has buoyed me up all the time. Last year when invading Maryland we were almost starved, and of course anyone would become disheartened. My health was never better than it is now, and I feel gay and jovial every way.

My brother Billie is out today guarding a man's premises. He was also out last night, and he told me this morning that they fed him splendidly. The reason houses are guarded is to prevent our troops plundering and robbing, which would demoralize them, thereby rendering them unfit for soldiers. Soldiers must have a strict and severe rein held over them; if not, they are worthless.

I have George's picture with me, and I look at it frequently.

RETREAT FROM GETTYSBURG.

Near Bunker Hill, Jefferson County, Va.,
July 17, 1863.

You will see by this letter that we have gotten back into "Old Virginia" again. It seems that our invasion of the North did not prove successful. We fought a dreadful battle at Gettysburg, Pa. It was the greatest battle of the war. We drove the Yankees three miles from the battlefield to a long range of high hills, from which it was impossible to dislodge them. General Lee had to fall back to keep them from getting the advantage. My brother was not hurt in the battle. Milton Bossard, Captain Cromer, Buford Wallace, Mr. Daniel's two sons and many others from Newberry were killed; but it is better for us all to be killed than conquered.

We have had some very disagreeable marching, as it has rained so much, but I have gotten hold of an old horse, which helps me along very much.

We have plenty of beef and bread to eat. We gathered up thousands of beeves in Pennsylvania—enough to feed our army until cold weather. This is a great consideration.

My servant got lost in Maryland. I do not think it was his intention to leave, but he was negligent about keeping up and got in rear of the army and found it too late to cross the river.

One of your letters came to me in Pennsylvania, and three since we left there.

We hear that Vicksburg has fallen. That is unfortunate, but I do not feel at all discouraged. Countries have been overrun, and then not conquered.

When we get settled down in camp again I will try to write you a longer and better arranged letter. We don't know what minute we may move, and under such circumstances I never can write with any satisfaction. I have George's picture yet. It is a wonder I did not lose it.

THE BATTLE OF GETTYSBURG

Camp near Orange Court House, Va.,
August 2, 1863.

In a recent letter I promised to write you more about our campaign in Pennsylvania.

On the night of the 29th of June we camped on the west side of the Blue Ridge Mountains, where they extend into Pennsylvania. On the morning of the next day (30th) we renewed our march. Shortly after starting it began raining, but the road was hard and well macadamized and the rain made the march rather agreeable than otherwise. On this same morning we passed where a splendid iron factory had been burned by General Early, of Ewell's Corps. It belonged to a very celebrated lawyer and politician of Pennsylvania by the name of Thaddeus Stevens, who is noted for his extreme abolition views and his intense hatred for slave-holders. The works are said to have been worth more than one hundred thousand dollars. The burning had thrown a great many operatives out of employment, and they seemed to be much distressed.

During the day we wended our way up the mountains. The scene around us was very different from what we had just passed through. Instead of the enticing field and lovely landscape, we had now around us that which was rugged, grand and towering. In the afternoon about one or two o'clock we halted and bivouacked among the mountains. Our stopping-place was in a basin of the mountains, which was very fertile and contained a few very excellent and highly cultivated farms. Awhile after we stopped I started off to one of these farmhouses for the purpose of getting my dinner, as I was quite hungry, and wanted something different from what I had been accustomed to most of the time on the march. On going to the house a very nice, smiling young girl met me at the door, and, upon my making known my wishes, she very pleasantly said she "guessed" so; but said they already had agreed to accommodate a good many, and that they would do the best they could by us all if I would return at four o'clock.

This I did, and found Adjutant Reedy of the Fourteenth Regiment and several others of my acquaintance. Reedy, being quite a young man, talked a good deal to the girl. I was hungry as a wolf, but when I came to the table and viewed what was upon it my hunger was aggravated more than ever. It seemed that there was no end to everything that was good. We had nice fried ham, stewed chicken, excellent biscuit, lightbread, butter, buckwheat cakes that were most delicious, molasses, four or five different kinds of preserves and several other dishes. We also had plenty of good coffee and cold, rich milk to drink. None but a soldier who has experienced a hard campaign can conceive of how a gang of hungry men could appreciate such a meal. I must say that this late dinner was a perfect Godsend.

After we had finished eating I felt ashamed to offer them Confederate money, but could do no better, and offered it with an apology. They very readily accepted it, and when I insisted that they should take a dollar they refused and would have only fifty cents. This house was guarded to prevent our men committing depredations such as they had been doing, and which was having a demoralizing effect upon the army. Soldiers must be made to behave or they will not fight.

Upon returning to camp I found that an order had been received during my absence to cook one day's rations and have it in haversacks and be ready to march at five o'clock next morning. This at once aroused our suspicions, for we concluded that we were about to meet the enemy. Next morning about five o'clock we began moving. We had not gone more than a mile and a half before our suspicions of the evening previous were fully verified and our expectations realized by the booming of cannon ahead of us in the direction of Gettysburg. Upon looking around I at once noticed in the countenance of all an expression of intense seriousness and solemnity, which I have always perceived in the faces of men who are about to face death and the awful shock of battle. As we advanced the cannonading increased in fury. It was Heth's Division, ahead of ours, fighting. At last we arrived upon a hill where, upon another hill in front of us and about a half mile distant, we could see Heth's cannon arranged and booming away at the Yankees, who were replying with considerable briskness, and we could also see the infantry of Heth's Division advancing in line of battle. It was really a magnificent sight. The country was almost destitute of forest and was so open that it was easy to see all that was going on. Our division (Pender's) continued to keep within about half a mile of Heth's. McGowan's Brigade was at the right of the division and the Thirteenth Regiment at the right of the brigade. This being the case, I could see from one end of the division to the other as it moved forward in line of battle. It was nearly a mile in length. The scene was certainly grand, taking all the surroundings into consideration. After Heth had driven the enemy some distance, it became necessary for our division to go to his support. McGowan's South Carolina and Scales's North Carolina brigades were the first to relieve Heth. The hardest fighting did not begin until McGowan's and Scales's divisions went into it. Then such a rattle of musketry I never heard surpassed. It lasted for about two hours and a half without cessation; and how many brave fellows went down in death in this short period of time! Officers who have been in all the fights tell me that they never saw our brigade act so gallantly before. When the order was given to charge upon the enemy, who were lying behind stone fences and other places of concealment, our men rushed forward with a perfect fury, yelling and driving them, though with great slaughter to themselves as well as to the Yankees. Most of the casualties of our brigade occurred this day (July 1). As the enemy were concealed, they killed a great many of our men before we could get at them. There were a good many dwellings in our path, to which the Yankees would also resort for protection, and they would shoot from the doors and windows. As soon as our troops would drive them out, they would rush in, turn out the families and set the houses on fire. I think this was wrong, because the families could not prevent the Yankees seeking shelter in their houses. I saw some of the poor women who had been thus treated. They were greatly distressed, and it excited my sympathy very much. These people would have left their houses, but the battle came on so unexpectedly to them, as is often the case, that they had not time. I passed through a house from which everyone had fled except an extremely old man. A churn of excellent buttermilk had been left, and I with some other doctors helped ourselves. Someone near by shot at us as we came out and barely missed us.

The fighting on the first day ceased about night, and when our brigade was relieved by Lane's North Carolina Brigade it was nearly dark. I returned to the hospital, and on my way back came to Anderson's Division of our corps (Hill's) lying in line of battle at least two miles in rear of where the advance column was. Pender's Division and Heth's had been fighting all day, and they were exhausted, besides being terribly "cut up"; and when they drove the Yankees to the long high range of hills, which the Yankees held throughout the fight, they should have been immediately reinforced by Anderson with his fresh troops. Then the strong position last occupied by the enemy could have been taken, and the next day when Ewell and Longstreet came up the victory completely won. If "Old Stonewall" had been alive and there, it no doubt would have been done. Hill was a good division commander, but he is not a superior corps commander. He lacks the mind and sagacity of Jackson.

When I arrived at the hospital my ears were greeted as usual at such time with the moans and cries of the wounded. I went to work and did not pretend to rest until next morning after daylight. I found that Longstreet had come and that McLaw's Division of his (Longstreet's) corps was encamped near the hospital. Kershaw's Brigade was almost in the hospital grounds. On looking around I discovered many of my old friends from Laurens whom I had not seen since the war began. They all seemed surprised and glad to see me; but I had work to do and they had fighting, so we could not remain long together. They were all lively and jocose. Milton Bossardt was in a gay humor and left me as one going on some pleasant excursion, but before two o'clock of the same day he was a corpse. He was shocked to death by the bursting of a shell. Captain Langston and a number of others in the Third Regiment who were my acquaintances were killed.

On the second day of the battle the fighting did not begin until about twelve or one o'clock, from which time until night it raged with great fury. The reason it began so late in the day was because it required some time for Ewell and Longstreet to get their forces in position. Longstreet was on the right, Ewell on the left, and Hill in the center.

On the third day the fighting began early in the morning and continued with the greatest imaginable fury all day; at one time, about three o'clock in the afternoon, with such a cannonading I never heard before. About 150 pieces of cannon on our side and as many or more on the side of the enemy kept up one incessant fire for several hours. It was truly terrifying and was like heavy skirmishing in the rapidity with which the volleys succeeded one another. The roar of the artillery, the rattle of the musketry and the wild terrific scream of the shells as they whizzed through the air was really the most appalling situation that could possibly be produced. Our troops (Pickett's Division) charged the enemy's strong position, which they had now entrenched, but with no avail, although we slaughtered thousands of them.

On the night of the 3d General Lee withdrew the army nearly to its original position, hoping, I suppose, that the enemy would attack him; but they didn't dare come out of their strongholds, for well they knew what their fate would be if they met the Confederate Army of Virginia upon equal grounds. On the 4th our army remained in line of battle, earnestly desiring the advance of the Yankees, but they did not come. During this day the rain fell in torrents, completely drenching the troops. Awhile after dark we began to leave, but took a different and nearer route to the Potomac than the one we had just passed over. Though nearer, it was very rough and not macadamized, and the passing of wagons and artillery over it cut it up horribly and made it almost impassable. Yet over this road our large army had to pass. I was lucky enough to get into a medical wagon and rode until next morning. It rained nearly all night, and such a sight as our troops were next day! They were all wet and many of them muddy all over from having fallen down during the night. Billie looked as if he had been wallowing in a mud hole, but was in a perfectly good humor. On this day (July 5) we recrossed the Blue Ridge Mountains. Climbing the mountains was very tedious after so much toil, excitement and loss of sleep, but we met with no obstacle until we came to Hagerstown, Md., where we stopped on account of the Potomac's being too high to ford. While here the Yankees came up and our army was placed in line to meet them, but they did not dare to attack. In this situation we remained for several days with them in sight of us.

After a pontoon bridge was finished at Falling Waters and the river was sufficiently down to ford at Williamsport, we left the vicinity of Hagerstown. It was just after dark when we began leaving. It was a desperately dark night and such a rain I thought I never before knew to fall. I did not meet with such luck as the night we left Gettysburg, Pa., but had to walk all night, and such a road I think troops never before traveled over. It appeared to me that at least half of the road was a quagmire, coming in places nearly to the knees.

Hill's Corps went by Falling Waters and Longstreet's and Ewell's by Williamsport, where they had to wade the river, which was still very deep, coming up nearly to the shoulders. The pontoon bridge was at Falling Waters, where we crossed. Our division was in the rear at this place, and when we got within about a mile and a half of the river we halted to enable the wagons ahead to get out of the way. Being very tired, we all lay down and nearly everyone fell asleep, when suddenly the Yankee cavalry rushed upon us, firing and yelling at a furious rate. None of our guns were loaded and they were also in a bad fix from the wet of the previous night. They attacked General Pettigrew's North Carolina Brigade first. Our brigade was lying down about fifty yards behind his. I was lying down between the two brigades near a spring. General Pettigrew was killed here. I was close to him when he was killed. It was a serious loss to the service. We fought them for some time, when General Hill sent an order to fall back across the river, and it was done in good order. The attack was a complete surprise and is disgraceful either to General Hill or General Heth. One is certainly to blame. The Yankees threw shells at the bridge and came very near hitting it just as I was about to cross; but, after we were close enough to the river not to be hurt by our own shells, our cannon on this side opened upon them, which soon made them "skedaddle" away.

We feel the loss of General Pender in our division. He died in Staunton, Va., from wounds received at Gettysburg. He was a very superior little man, though a very strict disciplinarian.

PART IV

IN CAMP AFTER GETTYSBURG CAMPAIGN— MILITARY EXECUTIONS—A STRATEGIC MOVE —RETURN FROM FURLOUGH—THE SEVERE WINTER—SCARCITY OF FOOD.

Camp near Orange Court House, Va.,
August 10, 1863.

All is quiet here now. When two armies have a great battle both sides are so crippled up that neither is anxious to fight soon again. The enemy must be somewhere about, or we would not be here. I do think there will not be another fight soon, for the Yankees dread us too much. It seems that Meade will not attack us, and that whenever we fight we must make the attack. I believe it will be a long time before we have another battle, if we have to wait for the enemy to advance on us.

Our long trip lately was very fatiguing, and we all became very thin and lean, although our health remained fine. Your brother tells me the Pioneer Corps had a very hard time of it on the way back from Pennsylvania. He took a more direct route to Culpeper Court House than we did, in order to assist some of Ewell's men in crossing the Shenandoah River.

Wilcox of Alabama is the major-general appointed over us, but he cannot surpass General Pender, who commanded us at Gettysburg. Pender was an officer evidently superior even to Hill. He was as brave as a lion and seemed to love danger. I observed his gallantry on the opening of the battle. He was mortally wounded on the first day as the fight was closing.

I have seen letters from some of our wounded who were left at Gettysburg. They are now in New York, and all say they are treated well. I had a chance to remain with our wounded, and, had I preferred to do so, I might have had a very interesting experience. Our chaplain, Beauschelle, was captured and is somewhere in Yankeedom, and I suppose is in prison, as chaplains are now held as prisoners, but he is apt to be released soon.

Our army is in splendid health and spirits, and is being increased rapidly every day by conscription and by men returning from the hospitals. Last year when a soldier was sent to a hospital he was expected to die, but all who come from the hospitals in Richmond now are highly pleased with the treatment they received. The hospital sections set aside for officers are admirably kept.

We get plenty to eat now and I am beginning to get as fat as ever again. Beef, bacon and flour, and sometimes sugar and potatoes, are issued to us. Dr. Tyler and I have obtained twenty pounds of sugar, a fine ham and one-half bushel of potatoes, and we hope to get some apples and make pies, as we have so much sugar. Vegetables are abundant in the country around here, and I succeeded in getting so much black-berry pie to eat recently that it made me sick.

Our regiment is on picket duty today. It went on last night. The weather is intensely hot, as hot as I ever experienced in South Carolina, but we are encamped in a fine grove and do not suffer from the heat as we would if marching.

The first chance I have I will send you two hundred dollars. You must buy everything you need, even if calico does cost three dollars a yard and thread one dollar a spool.

I am extremely gratified to hear that you and George are both in such excellent health, and I am glad you had him baptized.

Camp near Orange Court House, Va.,
September 1, 1863.

We still remain quiet in our old camp, with no sign of an enemy anywhere. I see no indications of our leaving here soon, but there is no telling. It is unreasonable for us to suppose we shall not have another battle here this summer. Old Lee is no idler; and, if the Yankees do not push a battle on him soon, he is almost sure to push one on them.

A little fellow returned to our regiment a few days ago who had made his escape from the Yankee prison at Fort Delaware. He traveled all the way back at night, and during the day kept safely hidden and rested. He had a most thrilling experience, which was full of just such hair-breadth escapes and wonderful adventures as I used to read about in histories when I was a boy, but which I did not believe at that time. I can believe them all now, for I see just such things occurring with us almost daily.

My new servant, Gabriel, arrived yesterday from South Carolina, and he seems well pleased so far. My brother and I had a great many questions to ask him about home. Billie is just like he used to be—fond of making fun of people. He wanted to know if Gabriel kissed Malinda when he left her, and he joked him about a great many things. Gabriel bought a watermelon in Richmond and brought it to us. It is the first one we have tasted in two years.

I got a new pair of shoes from the Government for six dollars. Billie's shoes are good yet, because I lent him a pair of mine to march in, and he wore them out and saved his own. Marching on these turnpike roads is very hard on shoes, and our army becomes barefooted in a short time.

We are living just as well as we could wish. I bought a bushel of potatoes yesterday, and we have plenty of meal, some flour, one ham and some rice.

Camp near Orange Court House, Va.,
September 16, 1863.

For two or three days we have been expecting another fight, and we had three days' rations cooked and were ready to move. It now appears that the Yankees have all gone back and that they sent only their cavalry forward. We have a very strong position here, and it is doubtful if they will advance this way. I am inclined to think that we shall soon begin to maneuver for the autumn campaign. It is reported that Longstreet's Corps had orders to move, and it was thought that it would be sent to the Army of the West. A part of it has gone off somewhere, and some of Ewell's troops were also moving recently.

Two men will be executed in our division next Saturday for desertion, and the entire division will be ordered out to witness it. I have never cared to witness a military execution, although I have been near enough several times to hear the report of the guns. Two men deserted from our regiment two nights ago, and, if we get them again, and this we are apt to do, they are sure to be shot. There is no other way to put a stop to desertions.

We have a large number of preachers here now from home, who are preaching to the soldiers, and we have religious services in camp almost every day.

Lieutenant-Colonel Hunt's wife is here to see him. Many others—wives of privates as well as officers—have come to visit their husbands. I think this is a very unsuitable place for women. If a battle should occur unexpectedly, they would all be in a nice fix.

My furlough has not been returned, but it has not had time, and it would also be delayed by the "rumpus" that the Yankees have just stirred up. I do not hope to have it approved now, but I am very apt to get home before Christmas. I have nothing more to tell this time, so good-bye to you and little George.

MILITARY EXECUTIONS

Camp near Orange Court House, Va.,
September 27, 1863.

We had nine more military executions in our division yesterday—one man from Thomas' Brigade, one from Scales' and seven from Lane's. Colonel Hunt was a member of the court-martial which sentenced them, and he tells me that one of the men from Lane's Brigade was a brother of your preacher, and that the two looked very much alike. He said he was a very intelligent man, and gave as his reason for deserting that the editorials in the Raleigh Standard had convinced him that Jeff Davis was a tyrant and that the Confederate cause was wrong. I am surprised that the editor of that miserable little journal is allowed to go at large. It is most unfortunate that this thing of shooting men for desertion was not begun sooner. Many lives would have been saved by it, because a great many men will now have to be shot before the trouble can be stopped.

We have been having some cavalry fighting recently. On the 23d the enemy were threatening to flank us, and our division was moved about six miles up the Rapidan River, but we soon returned to a place near our old camp. We have heard nothing of General Meade for the last few days, but we all expect soon to have a battle.

I must close, as a doctor has just come for me to go with him to assist in dissecting two of the men who were shot yesterday.

A STRATEGIC MOVE

Camp near Rappahannock River,
Culpeper County, Va.,
October 20, 1863.

This is the first chance I have had to write to you since we started on our autumn campaign. We have succeeded in maneuvering Meade entirely out of Virginia, as you must have already learned. The infantry did not have much fighting to do at any time on the entire trip, but the cavalry fought a large part of the time. Two North Carolina brigades became engaged with the enemy late one afternoon near Bristow Station, and our side got rather the worst of it. It was all due to the miserable management of General Hill or General Heth, or possibly both of them. The next morning the Yankees were gone, as they did not dare give battle to General Lee.

We have had a pretty hard time of it for the last few days on account of so much rain. It made the marching extremely disagreeable, but I stood the trip well, and enjoyed the best of health. Today the weather has cleared and it is bright and pleasant.

We have destroyed the railroad between Manassas and this place, so the Yankees cannot advance by that route again this winter, and I am sure the Army of Virginia will do no more fighting this year. Some part of it is sure to be sent somewhere soon, and our corps might go to Tennessee after resting a few days, or it might possibly be sent to General Bragg.

The part of Virginia through which we have marched has been totally devastated. It is now nothing but one vast track of desolation, without a fence or a planted field of any kind. I do not understand how the people exist, yet they do actually continue to live there. They are intensely hostile to the Yankees, and there is certainly no submission in them. If the people at home, who know nothing of the war, but who are always criticising the bad management of our general, could see these lofty-minded Virginians, who have lost everything but their proud spirit, they surely would hush and try to do something for their country.

Camp near Rappahannock River,
Culpeper County, Va.,
October 28, 1863.

There was a cavalry fight across the river yesterday, and I am told that we whipped them and took three hundred prisoners. We have been taking so many prisoners recently that we must be up with the Yankees again, or we may even have more of them in prison than they have of our men. We now have no prospect of a fight on a grand scale, and I suppose we shall go into winter quarters before much longer.

Old Jim Beauschelle, our chaplain, is out of prison and is back with us again. He was at Fort Delaware awhile, and was then sent to Johnson's Island in Lake Erie. He looks better than I ever saw him. He has a new hat, new shoes, and everything new, and looks like a new man. He speaks very highly of the Yankees and the way they treated him and of the good fare they gave him. He seems perfectly delighted with the North and the Yankees. I am sorry they did not handle him rather roughly and cure him of his wonderfully good opinion of them.

Your brother tells me you look better than you did before you were married. He says George is badly spoiled and that he will cry if you crook your finger at him. I am sorry to hear that he has been sick. In your letter you speak of his being pale and thin from teething.

I now feel quite sure that I shall be able to get home before much longer, but don't look for me until you see me walk in.

RETURN FROM A FURLOUGH

Richmond, Va.,
December 17, 1863.

I was delayed about ten hours at Charlotte, N. C., and did not arrive in Richmond until seven o'clock this morning. The weather was very agreeable for traveling and I had no trouble with my trunks.

I ate but once out of my haversack the whole way here. My appetite was gone, for the death of our dear little George, together with parting from you in such deep grief, made me sadder than I ever felt before in all my life. The heaviest pang of sorrow came upon me when I entered the train to leave. Since my arrival here the excitement of the city has revived my spirits somewhat. I visited both houses of the Confederate Congress today and saw Colonel Orr and others from our State, and also the distinguished men from other States.

I have no fear that there will be any trouble about my staying over my furlough. Had I remained at home a week longer not a word would be said. I shall go on to Orange Court House tomorrow and will write you a longer letter when I reach our camp.

THE SEVERE WINTER

Camp near Orange Court House, Va.,
January 3, 1864.

The cars ran off the track below Gordonsville yesterday, consequently we have no mail today. You do not know how anxious I am to hear from you. Your letters relieve the distress of my mind like a soothing balm placed upon a painful wound. I am sure I could forget the loss of our dearest earthly object much sooner if I could only be with you; but time will blunt the keenest thorns of anguish. I shall walk over and see your brother this evening if he does not come to see me before then. He was quite well when I last saw him, and had been busy repairing the roads.

The weather remains intensely cold, but the wind has abated somewhat today. I think yesterday was the coldest day I ever experienced, and it was made worse by the strong biting wind which blew incessantly. It is most severe on the wagoners and others who are out and exposed so much. When I saw the First South Carolina Regiment starting off on picket yesterday morning in the bitter cold I felt for them, but they seemed full of the life and vigor which the troops of Lee's army always display under the most trying circumstances.

I gave my old black coat to my brother. It fits him well and he is very much pleased with it. He has been keeping a chicken and it is now nearly grown, so we intend to have a big dinner soon, and will make a pot of dumplings and also have stewed corn and Irish potatoes.

I have been living in the same tent with Dr. Tyler. We slept together and were very comfortable, but I got a tent for myself yesterday and will have a chimney built to it and be ready to move in by the time he gets back. He and I are good friends and always get along very agreeably together, but he is too fond of drinking and gambling to suit me.

News is very scarce here now, and it would be difficult for me to write you a longer letter.

SCARCITY OF FOOD.

Camp near Orange Court House, Va.,
January 16, 1864.

The army is filling up with conscripts, absentees and others, and if we get also the principals of the substitutes our army will soon be very formidable. Mose Cappock has returned, although his wound has not quite healed. I believe if we whip the Yankees good again this spring they will quit in disgust. Their cause is not just, like ours, and they are sure to become discouraged more readily.

The people of Richmond have had a great time recently, feasting and fêting General Morgan. Men who saw him there tell me he is very young, handsome and attractive, but is modest and has a most pleasing address. I learned that when he passed through Newberry the people made him come out of the train and let them all take a good look at him.

An officer in our regiment was cashiered for forging a furlough, sure enough. I feel very sorry for him and think he should go to the Yankees the first chance he gets, for he is ruined wherever this thing becomes known.

The winter has been unusually severe so far, but I am perfectly comfortable in every way, except that our diet is becoming anything else but bountiful or extravagant. We draw a little coffee and sugar occasionally. For breakfast this morning I had a cup of "Pure Rio," some ham, rice, biscuit and butter, but I have a hankering for such things as syrup, sweet potatoes, sauer-kraut, and the like. I do hope it will not be a great while before I can have such things.

Edwin still has some of the good things to eat which he brought from home in his trunk. His servant, Tony, stole some of his syrup to give to a negro girl who lives near our camp, and Ed gave him a pretty thorough thrashing for it. He says Tony is too much of a thief to suit him and he intends to send him back home. I had to give Gabriel a little thrashing this morning for "jawing" me. I hate very much to raise a violent hand against a person as old as Gabriel, although he is black and a slave. He is too slow for me, and I intend to send him back by Billie when he goes home on furlough.

I must close, as Gabriel is bringing in my dinner. I will write to you again in a few days.

A BOX FROM HOME

Camp near Orange Court House, Va.,
January 30, 1864.

The weather has been fine recently and there have been some indications of a move. Yesterday we were ordered to cook one day's rations and be ready to march, but it has turned very cold today and everything is quiet again.

About ten days ago I succeeded in buying some turnips and cabbage, and I found them most delightful for a change until our box from home arrived. Everything in it was in excellent condition except the sweet potatoes. It contained ten gallons of kraut, ten of molasses, forty pounds of flour, twelve of butter, one-half bushel of Irish potatoes, one-half peck of onions, about one peck of sausage, one ham, one side of bacon and some cabbage. I am expecting Edwin to visit me tomorrow and I shall offer him part of the kraut and some of the molasses, but he is so independent I am afraid he will not accept it.

I saw Colonel Hunt's wife yesterday, and she is the first lady with whom I have conversed since my return in December. He pays ten dollars a day board for himself and wife at a house near our camp.

Dr. Tyler has had his furlough extended twenty days by the Secretary of War, and will not return before February. I have been alone for over four weeks. I have had such a quiet time that I have been reading Shakespeare some recently. I received a letter from Robert Land's wife begging me to give her husband a sick furlough, and I told him to write her that if he could ever get sick again he certainly should go at once.

The postmaster is here and I must close.

Camp near Orange Court House, Va.,
February 8, 1864.

The Yankees advanced to the Rapidan River yesterday and we were ordered off to met them. After some little fighting, they retired. It was evidently nothing more than a reconnoitering party of cavalry. Today everything is quiet.

Billie and I are enjoying our box immensely—especially the sauer-kraut. Edwin was over again yesterday. He has been over three times this week. I am just as comfortable in every respect as I could possibly wish to be. The health and spirits of everybody seem to be excellent.

I had my hair cut today and I feel quite cool about the head. I am sending you the soldier's paper which I take, and you will find it interesting. We have such a dearth of news that I do not know of one thing worth relating.

Camp near Orange Court House, Va.,
April 19, 1864.

We are still in camp, but yesterday we received an order to send back all surplus baggage and be ready to move at any time. No doubt we shall soon have a very interesting time of it and the papers will then be full of news.

General Longstreet's army is at Charlottesville. He may come here or go to the peninsula. That of course will depend on circumstances. All the news we received yesterday was very encouraging. The capture of Fort Pillow by Forrest was excellent for us. Gold is now 179 in New York, but if we whip Grant we may send it up to 300 for them.

I was glad to hear that old Jim Beauschelle was at our home. My father is decidedly hostile to the preachers who stay at home and preach to the women and old men, but I know he treated Beauschelle like a prince. If you see a certain widow, you might take the liberty of teasing her a little about old Beauschelle. She sent him some nice warm articles of clothing recently.

I have just finished my breakfast. I had corn bread, meat, molasses and coffee. Such a meal is first-rate for soldiers, but if the same were offered me at home I should feel like turning up my nose at it.

Orange Court House, Va.,
May 4, 1864.

We are still in our old camp. It may be some time yet before we have a big fight, although it can't remain off a great while, for the weather is fine and the roads are good.

Dr. Tyler leaves this morning for Richmond, and Dr. Kilgore will not come; so I am alone. I have very little to do, as there is scarcely any sickness. If we get into a battle soon I will have a tight time, but I hope to have someone with me before then.

The impression prevails that General Lee intends to act on the defensive this time. It is said that he is full of confidence. If the Yankees take Richmond it will be after they are cut to pieces. I can't believe they can ever possibly take it with this army opposed to them.

We had a pretty shower a few evenings ago. A considerable storm accompanied it and tents were blown about, but mine stood up through it.

My servant, Alick, is making a great deal of money washing for the soldiers.

PART V

BATTLE OF WILDERNESS—THE "BLOODY AN-GLE"—AT PETERSBURG—CHAFFIN'S BLUFF—PETERSBURG AGAIN.

BATTLE OF THE WILDERNESS.

Wilderness,
May 7, 1864.

On the 5th we marched all day on the plank road from Orange Court House to this place. We got into a hard fight on the left of the road rather late in the afternoon. The fighting was desperate for two or three hours, with the least cannonading I have ever heard in a battle. I suppose this was due to the level country and the thick undergrowth. It is low, flat and entirely unfit for cultivation.

After night Major Hammond rode up to where we doctors were and told us that about two miles to the rear there was a poor Yankee who was badly wounded. He insisted that someone of us go back to help him. I went, and found him paralyzed from a shot in the back. I gave him water and morphine, and made him comfortable as best I could. The poor fellow seemed very grateful.

After I returned to our lines the order came to move back with our medical stores to Orange Court House. We marched nearly all night, but just before day we were ordered back to the Wilderness again, and we reached there soon after sunrise. Longstreet came up about this time, having made a forced march all night. Then the fighting began in earnest—continuing fearful and desperate all day. The tremendous roar of the artillery and the rattle of the musketry seemed to make the woods tremble.

Late in the afternoon of this day I went among the wounded of the Third Regiment South Carolina Volunteers and of the Yankees who had fallen into our hands. As usual on such occasions groans and cries met me from every side. I found Colonel James Nance, my old schoolmate, and Colonel Gaillard of Fairfield lying side by side in death. Near them lay Warren Peterson, with a shattered thigh-bone, and still others who were my friends. Many of the enemy were there. Not far from these was an old man, a Yankee officer, mortally wounded. I learned that he was Brigadier-General Wadsworth, once Governor of New York.

I picked up an excellent Yankee overcoat on the battlefield, but the cape is off. I will have a sack coat made of it. I also found an India rubber cloth that is big enough for four men to lie on or to make a tent of. I have never before seen a battlefield so strewn with overcoats, knapsacks, India rubber cloths and everything else soldiers carry, except at Chancellorsville. The dead Yankees are everywhere. I have never before seen woods so completely riddled with bullets. At one place the battle raged among chinquapin bushes. All the bark was knocked off and the bushes are literally torn to pieces.

Tell Bob that as soon as I draw some of the new issue I will send him the pay for your cat-skin shoes.

[NOTE.—After two days of hard fighting at the Wilderness and the same at Spottsylvania, and failing to break through the Confederate lines, General Grant decided to make one more determined effort by concentrating in front of the angle in the Confederate breastworks. About daylight on May 12 a desperate charge was made upon this angle, which was occupied by General Bradley T. Johnson of Maryland. This overwhelming charge by the enemy was too much, and the Confederates were borne down, and General Johnson and his command of four thousand men and twenty pieces of artillery were captured. General Lee was in the rear with a reserve force, consisting of McGowan's South Carolina Brigade and some Mississippians, whom he rushed forward, and they reoccupied the angle. The Federals jumped back over the works, but did not retreat, and, after fighting all day and a greater part of the night, both sides were utterly exhausted, and ceased. A large oak standing on the works was cut down by bullets alone.]

DEFENSE OF THE BLOODY ANGLE

Field Hospital near Spottsylvania Court
House, Va.,
May 13, 1864.

When I wrote to you on the 7th instant I thought our fighting was over, for we had driven the Yankees off the field at the Wilderness and they had refused to attack us again; but we had another big fight with them the next day (8th instant) near this place. Then on the 10th another big fight here, and then one again yesterday that was the most terrific battle I have ever witnessed. The musketry and cannon continued from daybreak until night. Nothing that I have ever before heard compared with it. We were behind breastworks, but the Yankees charged into them in many places, fighting with the greatest determination, and it strained us to the utmost to hold our own. Such musketry I never heard before, and it continued all night, engaged with our brigade. It was perfectly fearful. I never experienced such anxiety in my life. It was an awful day, and it seemed to me as if all the "Furies of Darkness" had come together in combat. Everybody who was not firing was pale with anxiety, but our noble soldiers stood their ground, fighting with the utmost desperation.

The Yanks certainly tried their best yesterday, and they made us try our best too. It was the most desperate struggle of the war. I do not know that it is ended, but we have quiet today. I have not heard, but I hope the Yankees are gone and that I shall never again witness such a terrible day as yesterday was.

My brother passed through it all untouched. His company lost four killed, besides many wounded. John Landrum was killed and Scott Allen badly wounded. Mrs. Miriam Hunter's husband is mortally wounded. General Abner Perrin was killed, Colonel Brockman lost his arm, Captain McFall his eye, and General McGowan was severely wounded in the arm. This makes the fifth time he has been wounded. You will see all about it in the papers. I saw your brother Edwin yesterday. He was well, but, like everyone else, very anxious.

I will try to write you a longer letter when my mind gets settled.

Field Hospital near Spottsylvania Court
House, Va.,
May 17, 1864.

I received your letter of the 3d inst. this morning. You express regret that I do not receive your letters. I do receive them regularly, but you evidently do not receive mine.

We are still in "statu quo," the two armies confronting each other. I expect you know as much about the situation—or more—than I do, for, although we are right here, we know nothing unless we see the newspapers. I sent a telegram to Father on the 7th inst. from Orange Court House that my brother Billie had passed through the battle of the Wilderness safe.

We left there late that afternoon for Spottsylvania. I went over part of the battlefield as we were leaving, and saw that the Yankees had not taken time to bury their dead except behind their breastworks. We had no breastworks as far as I could see. In hurrying on we double-quicked much of the way. I understand that the dead are very thick on the battlefield near this place.

The weather cleared off yesterday, but it looks like rain again today. I never was more tired of rain. We all still have plenty to eat.

Between Chickahominy and Pamunky
Rivers, Va.,
June 1, 1864.

Your letters of the 24th and 26th ult. both reached me last night. The mails seem to be more regular now than for some time past.

There was not much fighting yesterday. It was only skirmishing. A few men were wounded in our brigade, only one of them being in my regiment. About an hour ago I heard heavy musketry on the extreme right of our lines, but it was far to the right of our division. We have every confidence that we shall be able to hold Richmond this summer. General Lee has an enormous army here now, and we all hope that Grant will attack us as soon as possible.

Jack Teague wrote me that Jim Spearman had been conscripted and assigned to light duty. Jack is very anxious for me to return to South Carolina as soon as possible, but it is no use to hand in a resignation at such busy times as these. I may send it in, though, whenever we get quiet again, so that it will be attended to. The longer I delay it the more apt it is to be accepted.

I was glad to know that you have the wool for my suit. I was proud of my old brown suit of last winter, but when I get a Confederate gray I shall be proud of it, sure enough. I have not drawn any money since last January, but as soon as I do I will replenish your purse. I should like so much to see your catskin shoes.

The weather is becoming quite warm. The dust is very bad and we are needing rain again. I have not seen your brother for several days, but suppose he is well. I have nothing more of importance to write at present, but will write you again tomorrow.

When I wrote to you two days ago I said appearances indicated that we were about to have a fight. Sure enough, about half an hour after I had finished writing the battle began. Our division was engaged. McGowan's Brigade did not suffer much. It supported Wright's Georgia Brigade of Anderson's Division, and, as the men were not engaged, they had the privilege of lying down. Consequently most of the missiles passed over them. The brigade lost only thirty or forty, and the Thirteenth Regiment had but one killed and two wounded.

We were very successful. It is estimated that we killed and wounded about two thousand. We captured about the same number and four cannon. Our loss was about four hundred. We are still in our old position. There was heavy cannonading this morning on our extreme left. If there was any musketry, it was too far for me to hear it. Just as I began to write this letter I had two wounded men to come in. They were hurt by a shell early this morning.

I had my third mess of beans yesterday, and a big one it was too. I shall have rather a poor dinner today—only bread, meat and coffee. We have been getting enough coffee and sugar to have it twice a day ever since I got back from home in April.

The weather is becoming very warm and we need rain. It will soon be too hot for military operations.

When you write again tell me all the little particulars about yourself. You do not know how much it interests me.

Near Chaffin's Bluff, Va.,
July 6, 1864.

I have not written to you for several days because I knew a letter could not go South from here. In the recent raids by the Yankees they cut both the Weldon and Danville railroads. I do not know that the way is open yet, but I will write anyway.

We remained at Petersburg just two weeks and then came back here last Saturday night to relieve two brigades of Heath's Division which were here on picket duty. We had a very pleasant time while in Petersburg. I succeeded in getting plenty of vegetables to eat. The Yankees are shelling the city, but the shells do very little harm and have killed but few. The people are not at all frightened by them. I would often see young ladies sitting on their porches reading quietly while shells were occasionally bursting near by.

As soon as communication is established between Weldon and Petersburg I hope we can get our box from home. I suppose Edwin is still about Petersburg, improving the entrenchments. It now looks as if our army will have to lie in line of battle all summer to keep the Yankees back. Poor devils! How they do long for Richmond! Our minds are prepared to endure anything rather than submit to them, and the nearer they get to us the more determined we are not to yield. In the interior where there is no danger nearly everybody is whipped, and they should be ashamed of themselves.

I am of course anxious to see you, but it is impossible for me to get off now. In fact, nothing could tempt me at this time to abandon the army. However, I hope it will not be long before we can be together, and remain so.

Near Chaffin's Bluff, on James River, Va.,
August 8, 1864.

The weather for the last few days has been intensely hot. It is very dry, and I hope we shall soon have some rain. My health is excellent. We get plenty of blackberries, and all we need is plenty of sugar to go with them.

I expect we shall soon go back to Petersburg, but I am informed that Kershaw's Brigade and several thousand cavalry have left for the Valley. This indicates that the seat of war may soon be around Washington instead of Richmond. I hope we will not be sent to the Valley again, for I detest those tedious marches. However, I am willing to do anything to whip out the Yankees.

Matters are comparatively quiet at present, although we hear more or less cannonading somewhere every day. At this moment I hear the booming of cannon away down on the James River. We are so quiet now that we have nothing to think about but home and our loved ones.

Word was sent from the headquarters of Wilcox's Brigade to McGowan's that a negro was captured at Petersburg the day Grant's mine was sprung (July 30), who claims to belong to a medical officer of McGowan's Brigade. On the provost marshal's register is the name of "William Wilson of New York." He always claimed that to be his name. I believe it may be my servant, Wilson. If so, the remarkable part of it is that he was captured charging on our breastworks. If I get him, I shall regard him as something of a curiosity in the future.

I received more pay on the 5th, and will send you one or two hundred dollars. I sent Bob the ten dollars for your catskin shoes. I bought an excellent pair of pants from the quartermaster for $12.50. They are made of merino wool. We shall soon have some fine gray cloth issued to the brigade for officers' uniforms. There will not be enough for all, so we will draw lots for it. If I am lucky enough to get any, I will send it to you.

I am very anxious to get a long letter from you giving me all the news. When I can hear from you regularly and know that you are safe and well, I feel satisfied.

48

It seems that you have not received the bundles I sent to you. I sent some gunpowder home recently, and you should get some of it for your brother Jimmie, if he wants it.

You express some apprehension that I shall not be able to get home this fall. I will try very soon to get off, but if I am disappointed you can come on here. I believe our brigade will remain about Petersburg this winter, and if we do I shall make some arrangements for you to be with me. Those of us here who have no children have planned to have our wives come out here and be with us this winter. The greatest difficulty in a man's keeping his wife here is in finding enough for her to eat, but we intend to have supplies sent to us from home. You must begin to make arrangements to come and be ready between the 15th of November and Christmas, if I do not get home before that time myself.

Last Thursday afternoon we received orders to be in readiness to move to the north side of the James River, and at about nine o'clock that night we started. We traveled until about two hours before day, and were nearly to Drury's Bluff when we were ordered back because the Yankees were making a demonstration on our right. That afternoon (Friday) our brigade and Lane's North Carolina had a considerable fight on the right. We drove them nearly two miles to their breastworks. It was a nice victory for us and our loss was small. The Fifteenth Regiment lost eight killed on the field and had about twenty wounded. I have never before known so large a proportion to be killed. Spencer Caldwell was killed. Colonel Bookter of the Twelfth Regiment and three officers of the Thirteenth were killed—none that you know. Billie was in it, but was not hurt. His company had one killed and but one wounded. Lang Ruff's boys were both in it, but were not hurt. I saw them all this morning and everybody was in fine spirits.

Our cavalry had a fight yesterday afternoon on the extreme right, and it is reported that General Dunnovant was killed. We are expecting the Yankees to attack us again. Grant is evidently doing his best for Lincoln's election. He must have been heavily reinforced. I hope to hear good news from Forrest. If Sherman is forced away from Atlanta and we can hold Richmond this winter, I believe we shall have peace.

We need ten or fifteen thousand more men here, and we could easily get them if the able-bodied exempts would come on here, but they seem to have become hardened to their disgrace. If the South is ever overcome, the contemptible shirkers will be responsible for it. They should have seen our poor fellows Thursday night coming in wounded and bleeding and shivering with cold; but these very men who suffer and have often suffered in this way are the last ones to say surrender.

I received your letter on Thursday, but have not been able to answer it until now. The weather is beautiful this afternoon, but it has been wet and was very disagreeable the day we had the fight.

Near Petersburg, Va.,
October 12, 1864.

I have not received a letter from you for several days, as there seems to be something wrong with the mails again.

Grant has come to a dead halt before Petersburg and Richmond. It is believed that the next fight will take place across on the north side of the James River. The Richmond papers state that there is encouraging news from Georgia, but they will not tell us what it is, because they say they do not want Grant to find out about it. Hood may have Sherman in a tight place.

About twelve thousand men from Richmond have been sent into the trenches at the front. Many of them were in the Government service and many others were gentlemen of leisure. The authorities sent everybody. The police would capture men in all parts of the city and send them under guard to some point to be organized and put under the command of officers who happened to be in Richmond from the army. A man told me these officers were seized in the same way on the streets, and that the authorities would even send out and capture a colonel and put him in command of the whole battalion. A medical officer would sometimes be seized. He would plead that he was due at his command and that he was a noncombatant, but they would tell him he was the very man they needed to attend to the wounded. It delights soldiers to hear of these things. It does them good all over. The soldiers are accustomed to these sudden dashes at the front, but the miserable skulkers almost die of fright.

We are building chimneys and fixing up things in our camp as if we are to remain here. If I were sure of it, I would have you come out and stay with me awhile. It is useless for me to try to get off now while we are so tightly pressed.

I saw Billie this morning. I carried a haver-sack full of biscuits and ham to him. I will have ham, light bread and coffee for breakfast in the morning. I have been living well this year.

We have a new chaplain in our brigade named Dixon. I heard him preach yesterday, and he does very well. If Congress would pass a conscript law bringing the preachers into the army we could have chaplains. They have acted worse in this war than any other class of men.

We are having rain tonight and I am very glad to see it, for the weather was dry and the roads were dusty.

Near Petersburg, Va,
October 25, 1864.

I have a bright fire this morning. There is a nice chimney to my tent, which makes it almost as comfortable as a house. The regiment is on the extreme right of our lines, but is several miles from the field infirmary where I am stationed. The brigades are frequently shifted about, but I trust ours will remain where it is, because there is plenty of wood near by.

Everything is very quiet on the lines. I suppose you have heard of the defeat of General Early again in the Valley. He has not yet gained a single victory worth mentioning, and it is time we had a new commander there. We have a great many good fighters, but so few good generals. I am anxious to hear something from General Hood, for if he can whip Sherman at Atlanta the situation may be entirely changed.

The health of all the men appears to be about as good as if they were at home under shelter and with suitable diet. Our troops seem as happy and lively as men could be, although they get nothing to eat now but bread and meat. We have eaten nearly all the beef Hampton captured recently in rear of Grant's army, but we have received some from North Carolina which is very nice and tender.

Your brother Edwin is to be appointed a lieutenant in the Fourteenth Regiment. I took dinner with him yesterday. Lieutenant Petty, with whom he messes, had just received a box from home, and I fared sumptuously. My box has not yet arrived. Boxes now take about two weeks to reach here. Your brother had received his new suit from home. Billie is well and hearty, but he needs a new coat. These government coats are too thin for exposed duty.

I have a nice little Yankee axe, which is so light that it can be carried in a knapsack, but it just suits a soldier for use in putting up his little shelter tent or for making a fire. All the Yankees have these little axes, and many of our men have supplied themselves with them, as they have with almost everything else the Yankees possess.

Are you making preparations to come out here this winter? Colonel Hunt will have his wife to come out again, and a great many other officers are arranging for their wives to come on soon. Some of them are here already, but I think it best for you to wait until winter puts a stop to military operations. When we left the Rappahannock River last fall some of the officers carried their wives along by having them wrap up well and putting them in the ambulance; and if you were here and we had to move I could easily take you along that way. I want you to come just as soon as circumstances will permit, but this war has taught me to bear with patience those things which cannot be avoided and not to be upset when my wishes cannot be gratified.

Near Petersburg, Va.,
October 29, 1864.

I suppose you have heard how we whipped the Yankees on both this side and the north side of the James River. The killed and wounded fell into our hands here at Petersburg, and we have been attending to their wounded all day today. Our loss was very small. Wilcox's Division was occupying a part of our line that was not assaulted, and therefore it was not engaged. We now have strong hopes of being able to hold Petersburg and Richmond.

This war can never end until the fanatics, both North and South, are gotten rid of. They are influenced solely by their blind, senseless passions, and reason never enters their heads. It is always such discontented, worthless wretches who bring about revolutions. The North is still infested with such characters, and the South is not far behind. If we could get those hot-headed fools in South Carolina who composed that meeting at Columbia recently and put them in the army and get them all killed off, it would be much better for us. What a pity we cannot have them killed, but they cannot be made to fight. I do not believe that Boyce will fight a duel with such a man as Tradewell, for he must have more sense than to do that.

My box is not here yet. I will continue to keep on the lookout for it until it arrives. My dinner will soon be ready and I think it will be fine, for I shall have white cabbage, bacon, potatoes and biscuit.

As soon as I can I will send you one hundred and fifty dollars to pay your expenses in coming out. The Government owes me about five hundred dollars, which I hope to be able soon to collect. If you can come by the first of December you can remain at least three months, and I may be able to go back with you in March.

Near Petersburg, Va.,
November 3, 1864.

We are still quiet. Nothing is going on except the continual fighting of the skirmishers, which amount to little more than a waste of powder and lead, although a man gets killed or wounded occasionally. The Yankees are keeping very quiet since the thrashing they received recently at this place and in front of Richmond. They will be apt to keep quiet now for some time —possibly for the remainder of the winter.

We are having rain. It fell all night and continues today. Billie's big coat came just in time for this cold spell of weather. He is as fat as a bear. The health of our troops is excellent and the spirit of the army is as fine as can be.

We shall know in a few days who is elected President of the United States. In my opinion Old Abraham will come in again, and I believe it would be best for us. McClellan might have the Union restored, if elected. I should prefer to remain at war for the rest of my life rather than to have any connection with the Yankees again.

You ask me to see Captain Pifer. I will do so if I happen to be near where he is again. He is now on the other (north) side of the James River with General Lee.

A man by the name of Simeon Werts is going home today on sick furlough for thirty days, and I shall send this letter to you by him. I shall also send my father some smoking tobacco, which we have been drawing monthly as part of our rations, and I shall send Dr. Clark some rolls of blistering ointment which we captured from the Yankees at Chancellorsville. I have more of it than I could use in two years. He has been very kind to you and I wish I had something more I could send him.

Our box of provisions from home still holds out, and if you will hurry up and come on, we may have some of it left when you arrive. I have just finished my breakfast, which consisted of hash, potatoes, biscuit, molasses and coffee. I do not mind the war as long as I can have plenty to eat and comfortable quarters. Your brother is very anxious for you to come out, and I believe you will enjoy it here this winter. It is most unfortunate that we have been able to see so little of each other during the four years of our married life.

Near Petersburg, Va.,
November 28, 1864.

The mails seem to be greatly deranged again, for I have not heard one word from you in two weeks. These clerks in the postoffices are the contemptible imps of cowardice who seek all the soft and safe places. They should be placed in the ranks and made to fight, and their places given to the young ladies who are refugees from within the enemy's lines and who would be glad to secure such employment.

Everything is quiet here now—only an occasional gun. Kershaw's Division has come back from the Valley and is now on the north side of the James River. The Yankees have not shelled Petersburg for several weeks, and it is beginning to have quite an air of business.

Grant agreed to cease shelling the city if General Lee would agree to keep all government property out of it. I do not believe Grant will make a serious attempt soon again to take Richmond or Petersburg.

A man is going home today on sick furlough, and I shall send this letter by him to be mailed to you from Columbia. I am glad you have decided positively to come on to Virginia. I will have everything ready for you when you arrive and will try to make you as comfortable as possible while you remain.

It was well you left Petersburg when you did, for the very next day (April 2) our extreme right was attacked, and, as our line was very thin, it was easily broken. Billie was digging a rifle pit when some Yankees charged it and captured all who were at work on it, and he is now a prisoner.

During the day a few prisoners were brought back, and among them was a smoke-begrimed captain with gray hair. I invited him into my tent and gave him something to eat. He had been in some of the hardest fighting of the war, and he said to me: "You see these white hairs. When I came into the army they were all coal black."

As night came on many wounded were brought back to some huts lately occupied by soldiers, but now used by us as a hospital. Among them was Mose Cappocks, and I amputated his thumb. General Hill was killed.

The next day we began to leave, and there was continuous fighting. Our march soon developed into a disastrous retreat, and we were pushed to the extreme every hour of it for eight days. At Sailors Creek we were compelled to abandon our wagons, and they were burned. In one of them I had a new case of the finest surgical instruments. They had recently run the blockade and I hated to see them destroyed. General Kershaw and his young son were captured here. I saw some Yankee spies in gray uniforms marched along with us under guard. They had been captured in our lines, but the surrender occurring so soon afterwards saved them from being hung.

Our retreat was most trying, and when we reached Appomattox on the morning of the 9th General Gordon had a fight and captured a battery. Appomattox is in a basin with high hills on all sides. The Yankees seemed to have surrounded us, and their blue lines, with white flags here and there, came moving in slowly and silently. There was a report in the early morning that we had surrendered, and this made us think it might be true.

I heard some of our men yelling, and saw General Lee and his staff riding towards us, and as he stopped to dismount the men crowded around him to shake his hand and every man was shedding tears. Sad as was the sight, everyone felt relieved that it was all over.

The Yankees camped on the hills, and men from both armies went back and forth on apparently friendly terms. Their wagons, mules, harness and entire equipment was the very best and everything was in perfect condition throughout. All of their wagon covers were white and new. Ours made a sorry spectacle in comparison. I unhitched a little mule from an ambulance, and that afternoon Colonel Hunt, Lieutenant-Colonel Lester, Captain Copeland and I started together for South Carolina.

We had one little fly tent under which we slept at night. Bill Byers, wh was mounted on a tall, gaunt horse, joined us before we reached th Catawba River. Copeland's horse gave out and he continued with us o foot. The river was swift and deep at Island Ford, and in crossing only th face and ears of my little mule remained above the surface. We found farm house near by, where we stood before a blazing fire to dry. The peopl were very kind to us and gave us the best they had to eat, but our clothe were too dirty and vermin-infested for us to sleep in their houses, so w slept in the barns.

At one house where we stopped and asked for something to eat th man's wife was in a pitiful condition with cancer, but was without medicin to alleviate her suffering. I happened to have a bottle of morphine in m haversack, which I gave her and which was enough to last her for the sho time she could live.

We were three weeks on the way, and when I reached my father's hom nobody was expecting me. I was completely exhausted, but after getting o some clean, whole clothes and sleeping in a bed once more I felt greatly re freshed. Father has given me a good horse in exchange for my little mul and I hope to be rested enough to leave here day after tomorrow and g through the county in a buggy for you.

ADDENDA.

The following letter was picked up in Raleigh, N. C., April 13, 1865, an is given exactly as it was written:

"deer sister Lizzy: i hev conkludid that the dam fulishness uv tryin t lick shurmin Had better be stoped. we hav bin gettin nuthin but hell & lo uv it ever sinse we saw the dam yankys & i am tirde uv it. shurmin has lots of pimps that dont care a dam what they doo. and its no use tryin t whip em. if we dont git hell when shirmin starts again i miss my gess. if cood git home ide tri dam hard to git thare. my old horse is plaid out or id trie to go now. maibee ile start to nite fur ime dam tired uv this war fu nuthin. if the dam yankees Havent got thair yit its a dam wunder. Tha thicker an lise on a hen and a dam site ornraier. your brother jim."

www.ingramcontent.com/pod-product-compliance
Lightning Source LLC
Chambersburg PA
CBHW011746020426
42331CB00014B/3295

* 9 781667 661810 *